the tornado detective

Exploring the Science of Tornados

sarah michaels

contents

introduction

Emily stared out of her bedroom window, her eyes wide with wonder. The sky, a vast canvas, was painting a picture she had never seen before. Dark, swirling clouds rolled in like waves on a stormy sea, and the wind sang a haunting melody that echoed through the old oak tree in her backyard. It was a regular afternoon in Oakville, a small town where everyone knew each other, and nothing extraordinary ever seemed to happen. But today was different. Today, the sky had a story to tell.

She remembered her grandfather talking about the weather, how it was like a moody artist, always changing its mind. Sometimes it painted in bright, cheerful yellows and blues, and at other times, it chose grays and deep, ominous blacks. Today, it seemed to be experimenting with the latter.

As Emily watched, fascinated, her younger brother, Max, burst into the room, his toy airplane in hand. "Emily, look! The sky is doing weird stuff!" he exclaimed, pointing excitedly towards the window.

"I see it, Max. It's a storm coming," Emily said, her voice a mix of awe and a slight hint of worry.

Their mother called from downstairs, "Kids, come away from the window. We need to get to the basement; a tornado might be on its way."

Tornado. The word sent a shiver down Emily's spine. She had read about tornadoes in her science book. Swirling, powerful columns of air, capable of lifting houses and tossing cars like they were toys. But reading about them and seeing the sky prepare to make one were two entirely different things.

Gathering Max and his toy plane, Emily hurried downstairs, following her mother to the safety of their basement. It was a cozy space, filled with old furniture and boxes of forgotten things. Her father had already turned on the small TV they kept there, the local weatherman's voice filling the room with urgent updates.

As they settled into the basement, Emily's thoughts raced. She remembered the chapter about tornadoes in her science book. How they formed when warm, moist air met cold, dry air, creating instability in the atmosphere. She imagined the air outside, dancing and twisting, getting ready to form a funnel.

"Why do tornadoes happen, Emily?" Max asked, his eyes wide and curious.

"It's like a battle between different kinds of air, Max. When they clash, it can create a tornado," Emily explained, trying to recall what she had learned.

"But why do they have to fight?" Max's question was innocent, yet it made Emily think. Nature, she realized, was full of forces that had to balance each other out. Sometimes, that balance was peaceful, and other times, it was as wild as a tornado.

As they waited, the sounds of the storm grew louder. The wind howled like a pack of wolves, and there was a distant rumbling that sounded like a giant walking over their town. Emily hugged Max a little tighter, trying to seem brave for her little brother.

Then, the weirdest thing happened. Amidst the chaos of the wind and the rumbling, there was a moment of eerie silence. It was like the storm was holding its breath. The weatherman on the TV called it the 'calm before the storm,' a brief pause before the tornado revealed itself.

Emily peeked through the small basement

window. She couldn't see much, but the sky had turned a strange greenish color. It was both beautiful and terrifying. She thought about the birds and squirrels outside, wondering where they took shelter during such a storm.

Suddenly, a funnel cloud appeared, descending from the sky like a giant, spinning finger. It was far away but visible from their basement window. Emily's heart raced. She was seeing a tornado for the first time.

"It's a tornado, isn't it?" Max whispered, his voice barely audible over the sound of the wind.

"Yes," Emily replied, her eyes fixed on the mesmerizing sight. "But it's far away. We're safe here."

They watched as the tornado moved across the land, its path unpredictable. Emily thought about how something so dangerous could also be so fascinating. It was nature's way of showing its power, reminding everyone that even in a small town like Oakville, extraordinary things could happen.

After what seemed like hours, the storm began to weaken. The wind calmed, and the tornado, having spent its energy, disappeared as quickly as it had formed. The sky cleared, revealing a rainbow that stretched across the horizon.

Emily and Max, along with their parents,

emerged from the basement. The air smelled fresh, like after a summer rain. Neighbors came out of their houses, checking on each other, sharing stories of the storm.

That night, as Emily lay in bed, she thought about the tornado. She realized that nature had its own language, a way of communicating through wind, clouds, and even tornadoes.

It was a language she wanted to understand more, to learn its secrets and wonders.

The tornado had been both scary and exciting, a reminder of the power and beauty of nature. Emily knew she would never forget the day the sky danced, the day she witnessed her first tornado. It was a day that had changed the way she looked at the sky, a day that had awakened a new curiosity in her heart. A curiosity about the world of weather, the mysteries of the atmosphere, and the endless stories the sky had to tell.

what is a tornado?

After the dramatic day when Emily and Max saw their first tornado, they were full of questions. What exactly was this spinning giant that had visited their town? To answer this, let's dive into the fascinating world of tornadoes, just like Emily and Max did, with a spirit of curiosity and wonder.

Imagine the sky as a giant playground, where different kinds of air play and sometimes, they don't play nice. Tornadoes are born from this playground, in a game involving warm, moist air and cold, dry air. But before we get into that, let's first understand what a tornado really is.

A tornado is like a spinning column of air that touches both the ground and the clouds above. It's not just any spin, though. It's a powerful whirl, so strong that it can lift things off the ground, twist massive trees, and even move houses. The part of the tornado we can see is actually made of water droplets, dust, and debris, all swirling around in a frenzy.

Now, how do these twisters come to life? It all starts with a special kind of thunderstorm, known as a supercell. Supercells are the mightiest of thunderstorms, with strong winds that go up and down, called updrafts and downdrafts. These winds are like the engines that power a tornado.

In these supercell storms, warm, moist air near the ground rushes up and meets cooler, drier air above. This meeting causes the warm air to cool down quickly, creating instability in the atmosphere.

It's like when you're playing with your friends, and suddenly someone starts a game you weren't expecting. The atmosphere gets all excited and charged up.

This excitement in the air causes it to spin horizontally. Picture a rolling pin spinning on a kitchen counter. Now, the updraft from the storm lifts this spinning air up into the clouds. Imagine someone lifting the rolling pin and standing it on its end. This is how the spinning starts to look like a tornado.

But not all spinning air becomes a tornado. It takes a special blend of conditions, like just the right temperature, humidity, and wind speeds. Think of it as a recipe. If you mix the right ingredients in the right way, you get a delicious cake. In the same way, when the atmosphere mixes its ingredients perfectly, a tornado is born.

Tornadoes come in different shapes and sizes. Some are thin and rope-like, twisting and turning as they move. Others are huge and wide, looking like giant, spinning cylinders. The size doesn't always tell you how strong a tornado is, though. Even a small, thin tornado can be powerful.

The center of the tornado is called the eye, and it's surprisingly calm, like the quiet eye of a hurricane. But it's surrounded by the fastest, most violent winds. These winds can reach up to 300 miles per hour, faster than race cars at full speed!

Tornadoes can be sneaky, too. They can come quickly and leave just as fast, sometimes in just a few minutes. Their paths are unpredictable, making them challenging to track. Scientists use radars and other tools to keep an eye on tornadoes, trying to warn people in time.

Now, you might be wondering, why do some places have more tornadoes than others? Well, it's all about location. In the United States, there's an area called 'Tornado Alley' that includes states like Texas, Oklahoma, Kansas, and Nebraska. Here, the conditions for tornado formation are just right, with lots of warm, moist air from the Gulf of Mexico meeting cold, dry air from Canada.

Tornadoes aren't just powerful; they're also one of nature's most incredible sights. People called storm chasers even follow tornadoes to study them and take amazing photographs. But remember, they are trained professionals with lots of experience. Tornadoes can be dangerous, so it's always best to respect their power and keep a safe distance.

Understanding tornadoes helps us prepare and stay safe when they happen. It also allows us to appreciate the incredible forces of nature. Just like

Emily and Max, who, after seeing their first tornado, began to look at the sky with new eyes, full of awe and respect for the whirling wonders of the world.

Tornadoes are a reminder of how amazing and powerful our planet can be. They show us that even in the wildest of weather, there's something to learn and marvel at. So next time you hear about a tornado, remember it's not just a scary twister, but a fascinating part of our natural world, a dance of air and energy that we're still learning about every day.

1 / the science of tornadoes

how tornadoes form

IMAGINE you're at a dance party. On one side of the room, you have warm, moist air, like dancers full of energy and warmth. They've come from places like the sunny beaches of the Gulf of Mexico, dancing and swirling around. On the other side, you have cold, dry air, more like cool, mysterious dancers from the snowy lands of Canada and the Rocky Mountains. When these two groups of air meet, they don't just mingle; they start an epic dance battle.

This dance starts with the warm air trying to move upwards. Warm air, being lighter and more buoyant, loves to rise. It's like a bunch of hot air balloons trying to float up into the sky. This warm air is full of moisture, which it picked up from the oceans and lakes. As it rises, it cools down, and the moisture turns into tiny water droplets, forming clouds. This is the beginning of our storm.

Meanwhile, the cold air, which is heavier and denser, does the opposite. It wants to sink down to the ground. Think of it as a group of cool, heavy bowling balls rolling along the floor. When the cold air pushes down, it forces the warm air to rise even faster. This is where things start to get interesting.

As the warm air rises and the cold air sinks, it creates a kind of rotation. Picture a giant, invisible spiral staircase in the sky, with the warm air going up and the cold air coming down. This rotation is the first step in creating a tornado, but it's not quite there yet. At this point, the rotation is horizontal, lying flat across the sky. What we need is for this rotation to turn vertical.

Enter the wind. Not just any wind, but winds that change speed and direction with height. These are called wind shears. Near the ground, the wind might be blowing gently from one direction, but higher up, it could be faster and from a different direction. This difference in wind speed and direction starts to tilt our horizontal rotation into a vertical one. Now, our tornado is beginning to take shape.

But there's more to this dance. The rising warm air, now full of moisture, keeps cooling down as it climbs higher. The moisture condenses into water droplets, creating clouds and releasing heat. This heat release makes the air even lighter and causes it to rise faster. It's like adding more energy to our dance, turning it from a slow waltz into a fast-paced tango.

This fast-rising air creates a powerful updraft, a strong current of air moving upwards in the storm. The updraft stretches the rotating air, making it spin faster, just like a figure skater pulling in their arms to spin faster on ice. This is the core of our tornado, where the most intense spinning happens.

As all these elements come together – the warm air rising, the cold air sinking, the wind shears tilting, and the updraft spinning – the tornado starts to form. It begins as a funnel cloud, a spinning cone of air hanging from the cloud base. When this funnel touches the ground, congratulations, you've got a tornado!

This entire process is a delicate balance. Not every thunderstorm creates a tornado; it takes just the right mix of warm air, cold air, moisture, and wind conditions. Scientists are still trying to understand all the details of this dance, studying storms to predict when and where a tornado might form.

Tornadoes are nature's way of balancing out the differences between warm and cold air. It's like the atmosphere's method of sorting out its differences, with a spectacular and powerful dance. While they can be dangerous, understanding how tornadoes form helps us prepare and stay safe.

different types of tornadoes

Think of tornadoes as artists, each creating a different kind of masterpiece. Some are slender and graceful, while others are wide and powerful. Some appear for a brief moment, and others seem to linger, leaving a lasting impression.

The first type we'll explore is the classic 'cone' tornado. These are the ones you might see in pictures or movies. They look like a giant funnel, wider at the top and narrower as they touch the ground. Imagine an elephant's trunk swinging down from the clouds. Cone tornadoes are the most common type. They're like the regulars at the tornado dance party, showing up more often than their peers.

Next, we have the 'rope' tornadoes. These are the slender, twisting types, looking like a rope or a snake dangling from the sky. Rope tornadoes are often the final stage in a tornado's life. As they start to lose energy, they stretch and twist, getting thinner and longer. Watching a rope tornado is like watching a dancer do a final, graceful pirouette before leaving the stage.

But not all tornadoes are so delicate. Enter the 'wedge' tornado. These are the giants, as wide or wider than they are tall. Picture a massive block of dark clouds, plowing across the land. Wedge tornadoes look incredibly powerful and can be some of the most destructive. They're like the heavyweight champions in the world of tornadoes, commanding awe and respect.

There's also a special kind of tornado called a 'waterspout.' These are tornadoes that form over water. Imagine a swirling column of air and mist, dancing over the ocean or a lake. Waterspouts are usually weaker than land tornadoes, but they're a spectacular sight, like a water ballet put on by nature.

In colder regions, there's a cousin to the waterspout called the 'snowspout.' These are rare and form in cold conditions over bodies of water. It's like seeing a waterspout dressed up in winter attire, swirling amidst snowflakes.

Now, let's talk about the strength of tornadoes. The power of a tornado is measured by the Enhanced Fujita Scale, or EF Scale. It ranges from

EF0, the weakest, to EF5, the strongest. The scale is based on the damage a tornado causes. An EF0 might just break some tree branches, while an EF5 can tear buildings off their foundations. It's like grading the tornadoes based on how much of a mess they make.

Despite their differences, all tornadoes form the same way, from the dance of warm and cold air. But the conditions they form in, like the amount of moisture in the air, the temperature, and the wind conditions, can influence their shape and size.

Sometimes, tornadoes like to show up to the party in groups. These are called 'tornado families' or 'tornado outbreaks.' Imagine several tornadoes, each taking its own path across the land. Tornado outbreaks can be particularly challenging for meteorologists to predict and track.

As Emily and Max learned about the different types of tornadoes, their fear turned into fascination. They realized tornadoes were not just random whirlwinds but part of the Earth's complex weather system. Each tornado, with its unique shape and size, was a reminder of the diversity and power of nature.

tornado alley

Tornado Alley isn't a real alley with buildings and streets. It's an area in the United States where tornadoes are more common than anywhere else in the country. This area includes parts of Texas, Oklahoma, Kansas, Nebraska, and South Dakota. It's like a special stage set up by nature, perfect for tornadoes to perform their swirling dances.

So, what makes Tornado Alley the ideal place for tornadoes? It all goes back to our dance of warm and cold air. Tornado Alley is like a meeting point for these different types of air. Warm, moist air comes up from the Gulf of Mexico, while cold, dry air comes down from Canada. When they meet in Tornado Alley, it's like the perfect dance party for tornadoes to form.

In the spring and early summer, Tornado Alley becomes particularly active. This is because the conditions are just right. The ground is warming up from the spring sun, and the air above is still cool from the winter. It's like the atmosphere is setting up a dance floor for tornadoes.

But what about the people who live in Tornado Alley? For them, life is a bit different. They're used to the sky changing quickly and always keep an eye out for stormy weather. Living in Tornado

Alley means being prepared. People here know what to do when a tornado warning is issued. They have safe rooms or storm cellars where they can take shelter. It's like having a special hiding spot for a game of hide-and-seek with the weather.

Schools and communities in Tornado Alley often have drills and practice what to do during a tornado. It's like a fire drill, but for tornadoes. This way, everyone knows how to stay safe when the sky starts to dance wildly.

Did you know that not all tornadoes in Tornado Alley are giant, destructive twisters? Many tornadoes here are small and don't last very long. But even the small ones are taken seriously because they can still be dangerous.

Meteorologists, the scientists who study weather, pay close attention to Tornado Alley. They use radars, satellites, and other tools to watch the storms that form here. This helps them warn people when a tornado might be on the way. It's like having a lookout in a tower, watching for danger and ready to sound the alarm.

People who live in Tornado Alley have learned to respect the power of nature. They know that tornadoes are a part of life here, like snow in the mountains or rain in the rainforest. They've adapted to their environment, building stronger houses and learning how to stay safe.

Tornado Alley isn't just about the danger of tornadoes. It's also a place of learning and discovery. Scientists come here to study tornadoes, trying to understand why they form and how they move. This research helps us all, because the more we know about tornadoes, the better we can prepare for them.

Tornado Alley is also a reminder of how incredible our planet is. It shows us that nature has its patterns and rhythms. Just like there are places where it's always snowy or always rainy, there are places like Tornado Alley where tornadoes are a part of the landscape.

fun facts

Tornadoes are not just powerful forces of nature; they're also full of surprises! In this section, let's spin through some fun and fascinating facts about tornadoes. These tidbits are perfect for dazzling your friends and family with your tornado knowledge.

First off, did you know that the United States is the tornado capital of the world? That's right! The U.S. has more tornadoes than any other country, averaging about 1,200 a year. That's a lot of twisters! Most of these occur in Tornado Alley, but tornadoes can happen in almost every state.

Now, let's talk about speed. Tornadoes can move really fast. They can travel across the ground at speeds of up to 70 miles per hour. That's faster than most cars drive on the highway! But when it comes to the speed of the winds inside the tornado, they can be even faster. The fastest tornado winds can reach over 300 miles per hour. Imagine trying to stand in winds that strong!

Here's something that might surprise you: not all tornadoes are visible. Sometimes, the funnel of a tornado doesn't have enough moisture or dirt to be seen. These invisible tornadoes can be especially dangerous because people might not know they're there.

Tornadoes can also come in different colors. The color of a tornado depends on what it's traveling through. If it's moving through a red dirt area, the tornado might look red. In other areas, it might appear gray or white. It's like a tornado's way of playing dress-up, changing colors based on its surroundings.

Did you know that the sun can influence tornadoes? Solar activity, like sunspots and solar flares, can affect the Earth's weather, including the formation of tornadoes. It's like the sun is joining in the dance of the atmosphere from millions of miles away.

Now, let's talk about water. When a tornado passes over a river, lake, or ocean, it can create a waterspout. Waterspouts are like tornadoes' cousins. They're usually weaker than tornadoes over land, but they can still be pretty strong. And just like tornadoes, they can lift water and fish from the sea and drop them on land. Imagine it raining fish – what a fishy surprise that would be!

Tornadoes have been part of history for a long time. The oldest recorded tornado happened in Ireland in 1054. That's almost a thousand years ago! Tornadoes have been whirling around long before we started keeping track of them.

Here's a cool fact about tornado safety: the safest place to be during a tornado is in a basement or an interior room on the lowest floor of a building. But did you know that opening windows to equalize pressure during a tornado is a myth? It doesn't help at all and can be dangerous. The best thing to do is to get to safety and stay away from windows.

Tornadoes can do some pretty strange things. They've been known to pluck feathers off chickens and strip bark off trees. They can drive straws into trees like nails and lift houses off their foundations. It's like they have a magical, if somewhat mischievous, power.

Did you ever wonder how long tornadoes last? Most tornadoes are on the ground for just a few minutes, but some can last for more than an hour. The longest-lasting tornado on record was on the ground for about 3.5 hours, traveling more than 200 miles. That's one long, tireless dance!

Lastly, let's talk about tornado sounds. People who have been near a tornado often say it sounds like a freight train. The loud, rumbling noise comes from the wind and debris swirling around at high speeds. It's like nature's orchestra playing a thunderous symphony.

2 / famous tornadoes in history

historical tornado events

THROUGHOUT HISTORY, tornadoes have danced their way across our landscapes, leaving both awe and destruction in their wake. Let's journey back in time and explore some of the most significant tornado events.

We'll start with the Tri-State Tornado, which happened on March 18, 1925. This tornado holds records that are still unbeaten today. It's the deadliest single tornado in U.S. history, with 695 people losing their lives. It traveled across three states - Missouri, Illinois, and Indiana - and was on the ground for a staggering 3.5 hours, covering 219 miles! Imagine a tornado as long-lasting and far-traveling as this one; it's almost hard to believe. The Tri-State Tornado was so powerful that it picked up houses and tossed them, leaving towns like Murphysboro, Illinois, and Griffin, Indiana, in ruins. This tornado taught us how far and fast tornadoes can travel and the importance of timely warnings.

Next, let's visit the town of Woodward, Oklahoma, on April 9, 1947. A massive tornado, part of a larger outbreak, struck this town and caused incredible destruction. It was a giant, a mile wide at times, and it turned homes and businesses into rubble. The Woodward tornado was a grim reminder of the power of nature, claiming 181 lives and injuring many more. It led to improvements in tornado forecasting and awareness, helping us be better prepared for future twisters.

Moving forward to May 3, 1999, we encounter the Oklahoma Tornado Outbreak. This series of tornadoes struck Oklahoma and Kansas, with one particularly devastating tornado hitting the city of Moore, Oklahoma. What made this tornado stand out was its incredible wind speeds, which were estimated at over 300 miles per hour. These were some of the highest wind speeds ever recorded on Earth. This event showed us just how extreme tornado wind speeds could get and spurred advancements in radar technology, helping meteorologists track and predict tornadoes with greater accuracy.

Another significant event was the Super Outbreak of April 2011. Over just three days, from April 25 to 28, a staggering 360 tornadoes touched down across the United States, from Texas to New York. It was one of the largest and most intense tornado outbreaks ever recorded. The city of Joplin, Missouri, experienced one of the most destructive tornadoes of this outbreak on May 22. With winds over 200 miles per hour, it tore a path of devastation a mile wide and left a scar on the city that is still visible today. The 2011 Super Outbreak was a stark reminder of the frequency and intensity of tornadoes and led to further improvements in emergency response and community preparedness.

• • •

Now, let's travel across the ocean to Bangladesh, which has experienced some of the deadliest tornadoes in the world. On April 26, 1989, a tornado struck the Manikganj District, killing over 1,300 people. This tragedy highlighted that tornadoes are not just a U.S. phenomenon; they can happen anywhere under the right conditions and can be just as deadly.

These historical tornado events are more than just stories from the past; they are lessons for the future. They teach us about the power of nature and the importance of being prepared. They show us the need for better warning systems, stronger buildings, and more research into how tornadoes work.

impact on communities

Tornadoes are more than just swirling columns of wind; they're events that can leave a lasting impression on the towns and cities they touch. In this chapter, we'll explore how tornadoes have impacted communities, transforming landscapes and lives in profound ways.

. . .

Picture a typical sunny day in a small town, with people going about their daily routines. Suddenly, the sky darkens, and a tornado appears on the horizon. In just moments, this powerful force of nature can change everything. Buildings that stood for decades can be destroyed, trees uprooted, and neighborhoods turned upside down. The physical impact is immediate and often devastating, but the story doesn't end there.

After a tornado passes, communities face the enormous task of rebuilding. This isn't just about repairing buildings; it's about restoring lives. People come together to help each other, showing incredible strength and resilience. Neighbors who were strangers before the tornado become friends in the aftermath, united in their efforts to rebuild.

Schools play a big role too. After a tornado, schools may serve as shelters or supply distribution centers. Teachers and students often work hand in hand to support recovery efforts. It's a time when the community's spirit shines brightest, showing that even in the darkest times, people can bring light to each other's lives.

. . .

Businesses in tornado-affected areas also face challenges. Some may need to rebuild entirely, while others find ways to adapt and continue operating. Local businesses are the heart of many communities, and their recovery is crucial for the town's overall recovery.

One of the most inspiring things about communities hit by tornadoes is how they come together to support one another. Fundraisers, food drives, and volunteer construction crews are common sights. It's a powerful reminder of the kindness and generosity that exists in people.

But it's not just about rebuilding what was lost. Many communities use the experience of a tornado to build back better. This might mean constructing stronger buildings, improving warning systems, or developing better emergency response plans. It's like learning a hard lesson from nature and using it to become stronger and more prepared for the future.

. . .

For kids like Emily and Max, seeing their community come together after a tornado can be a life-changing experience. It teaches them about compassion, teamwork, and the importance of community. They learn that even when something as scary as a tornado happens, there are always people ready to help and support each other.

Tornadoes also teach communities about the environment and the climate. They remind us of the power of nature and the need to respect and understand it. In some places, communities have started focusing more on environmental conservation and sustainability as part of their rebuilding efforts.

The impact of a tornado can last for years. The physical rebuilding might be completed, but the emotional recovery can take much longer. Communities often hold memorials or create monuments to remember the event and honor those who were lost or affected. These memorials serve as a symbol of the community's resilience and hope.

• • •

In addition to physical and emotional recovery, tornadoes can also bring about innovation. Scientists and engineers often work with communities to study tornadoes and develop new technologies to better withstand future storms. This can include stronger building materials, advanced warning systems, and more effective emergency response strategies.

As communities rebuild, they also retell their stories. They pass down the tales of survival, resilience, and unity to future generations. These stories become a part of the community's identity, a testament to their strength and perseverance.

The impact of tornadoes on communities is a complex tapestry of destruction and rebuilding, loss and healing, fear and courage. It's a story of how people, when faced with the incredible force of nature, respond with an even more incredible force of human spirit.

3 / tornado safety

safety measures

WHEN IT COMES TO TORNADOES, being prepared and knowing what to do can make all the difference. In this section, we're going to learn about safety measures to take during a tornado. Think of it as a guide to staying safe when the winds start dancing a little too wildly.

The first and most important thing to know about tornado safety is being aware. Awareness means keeping an eye on the weather, especially if you live in a place where tornadoes are common. Nowadays, we have apps and news channels that give us weather updates. It's like having a personal weather detective, letting you know when trouble might be brewing in the sky.

If a tornado watch is issued, it means conditions are right for a tornado to form. This is your cue to start getting prepared. Check your emergency kit (we'll talk about what should be in it a little later) and make sure you know where to go if a tornado warning is issued. A tornado warning means a tornado has been seen or picked up by radar. This is when you need to take action and find shelter.

The best place to be during a tornado is in a basement or storm cellar. If you don't have a basement, go to the lowest floor of your building. Find a small, windowless room like a bathroom or closet. It's like playing a game of hide-and-seek with the tornado, and you want to pick the best hiding spot in the house.

If you're in a school or office building, avoid large, open areas like gyms and cafeterias. These places have wide roofs that can be more easily damaged by tornadoes. Instead, find an interior hallway or a small room on the lowest floor. Stay away from windows, as they can shatter during a tornado.

Now, let's talk about your emergency kit. This kit should be like a treasure chest of items that can help you during and after the tornado. It should include water, non-perishable food, a flashlight, batteries, a first-aid kit, and a whistle to signal for help. You might also want to include a small radio to listen to weather updates and a phone charger.

If you're outside and can't get to a safe building, try to find a low-lying area like a ditch or a ravine. Lie flat and cover your head with your arms. It's not the ideal place to be, but it's better than being out in the open. Remember, never try to outrun a tornado in your car. They can change direction quickly and are much faster than you might think.

One thing that's really important during a tornado is to protect your head. Injuries from flying debris are common, so using helmets can be a life-saver. It might seem a bit odd to put on a bike helmet when you're inside, but it's a smart move when a tornado is nearby.

After the tornado has passed, be careful when you come out of your shelter. Watch out for debris and broken glass. If you're at home, use a flashlight to inspect your house for damage. If you smell gas or see downed power lines, leave the area immediately and let the authorities know.

If your community has been hit by a tornado, it's important to stay out of the way of emergency workers. They're like the superheroes who come in after the storm, and they need space to do their work. If you want to help, the best thing to do is to donate to reputable relief organizations.

emergency kits

When it comes to tornadoes, one of the best ways to be a superhero is to have a super-prepared emergency kit. Think of this kit as your treasure chest, filled with items that will help you during and after a tornado. Let's dive into what makes a great tornado safety kit, piece by piece.

First, imagine if the power went out during a tornado. How would you see in the dark? That's where your trusty flashlight comes in! A good, durable flashlight is like a beacon in the night, guiding you safely. Don't forget extra batteries, because even the best flashlight won't help if it runs out of power.

Next, let's talk about communication. A battery-powered or hand-crank radio can be your link to the outside world. It will keep you updated on the weather situation and any important announcements. It's like having a messenger bird that brings you news!

Water is essential. In your kit, you'll need enough water for at least three days. The rule of thumb is one gallon per person per day. Water isn't just for drinking; it's also for cleaning up any little cuts or washing your hands.

Food is next on the list. Pack non-perishable

items like canned goods (don't forget the can opener!), granola bars, and dried fruits. Think of foods that don't need cooking or refrigeration. It's like packing for a very important picnic.

Safety is crucial, so a first-aid kit is a must. It should include things like bandages, antiseptic wipes, adhesive tape, and pain relievers. It's like having a mini-doctor in a box, ready to take care of small injuries.

Sometimes, tornadoes can leave you in a situation where you need to signal for help. A whistle is perfect for this. It's small, easy to carry, and the sound carries far. Three blasts of a whistle is a well-known signal for help.

In case you need to leave in a hurry, have copies of important documents in your kit. These could include identification, insurance policies, and bank account records. Keep them in a waterproof container. It's like having a backup of your important papers, just in case.

Staying warm and dry is important, so include a blanket or sleeping bag. If space allows, add some extra clothes, especially socks and a warm hat. It's like packing for an unexpected sleepover.

Personal hygiene items are also important. Include things like toothbrushes, toothpaste, and moist towelettes. Staying clean can keep you feeling human even in tough times.

Don't forget about special needs. If someone in your family takes medication, make sure to have a supply in your kit. The same goes for baby supplies or pet supplies if you have little ones or furry friends in your family.

For a bit of comfort, especially if you have kids, include a small toy, book, or a deck of cards. These can be a welcome distraction and can help keep spirits up.

Lastly, keep your emergency kit in an easily accessible place. Make sure everyone in the family knows where it is. It's like having a map to a hidden treasure, only this treasure can help keep you safe.

seeking shelter

Imagine you're at home, and you hear a tornado warning. The first thing to remember is not to panic. Tornadoes can be scary, but being prepared and knowing where to go keeps you one step ahead. The best place to be is in a basement or an underground storm cellar. These are like hidden fortresses, deep in the ground, where the strong winds and flying debris can't reach you.

If you don't have a basement, don't worry. The next best place is a small, windowless room on the lowest floor of your home. Bathrooms, closets, and hallways can be good choices. The idea is to put as many walls between you and the tornado as possible. It's like building a fortress of walls around you. Stay away from windows, as they can shatter and cause injuries.

But what if you live in an apartment building or a high-rise? In that case, getting to the lowest floor is important. If you can't get to the ground floor, go to a hallway, bathroom, or closet in the center of the building. Avoid rooms with windows or large open spaces like gymnasiums or auditoriums.

Sometimes, you might be at school when a tornado warning is issued. Schools usually have a tornado safety plan, and it's important to follow it. Teachers and school staff will guide you to designated safe areas. These are often interior hallways or rooms without windows. Crouch down, cover your head with your arms, and stay as low as possible. It's like playing a game of turtle, tucking in and staying protected.

If you're in a shopping mall or large store, look for a designated shelter area or a small, windowless room or hallway. Avoid large, open areas like the main corridors of the mall. Remember, the key is to have as many walls between you and the tornado as possible.

What if you're caught outside with no shelter nearby? This can be a tricky situation. The best thing to do is to find a low, flat location away from trees and cars, like a ditch or a ravine, and lie flat, covering your head with your hands. It's not the safest place to be, but it's better than being out in the open.

Now, let's talk about mobile homes. If you live in a mobile home, it's really important to have a plan for where to go during a tornado. Mobile homes are not safe in a tornado, even if they're tied down. If a tornado warning is issued, leave your mobile home and go to the nearest sturdy building or storm shelter.

In communities where tornadoes are common, there are often public storm shelters. These are buildings designed to withstand strong winds and provide a safe space during a tornado. If you know where your nearest storm shelter is, that's a great place to go. If you're not sure, check with your local community center or government office.

Having a plan for where to go during a tornado is like having a map in a treasure hunt. It guides you to the safest place, so you're not left wondering what to do when a tornado is on its way.

4 / tornado researchers and storm chasers

meet the experts

IN THE FASCINATING world of tornadoes, there are some real-life superheroes who work tirelessly to understand these swirling wonders. They're not wearing capes or flying through the sky, but they are armed with knowledge, technology, and an undying curiosity about the weather. Let's meet the tornado experts – the scientists who study tornadoes and help keep us safe.

First up are the meteorologists. These weather wizards use their deep understanding of the atmosphere to predict when and where tornadoes might happen. They work with tools like weather radars, satellites, and computer models to track storms. It's like putting together a giant puzzle, where each piece is a clue about the weather. Meteorologists are the ones who issue tornado watches and warnings, helping to alert people to potential danger.

Next, let's talk about storm chasers. Yes, you heard that right – storm chasers! These are the brave (and a bit daring) scientists who actually follow tornadoes to learn more about them. Equipped with all sorts of gadgets, like anemometers to measure wind speed and video cameras to capture every moment, they head straight into the action. Their goal is to collect data and learn more about how tornadoes form and behave. It's like being a nature detective, solving the mysteries of the weather.

Then there are the engineers. These problem-solvers look at the damage caused by tornadoes and figure out how to make buildings stronger and safer. They study things like how different structures stand up to strong winds and what materials work best in tornado-prone areas. Their work helps make sure that homes, schools, and other buildings can better withstand the fury of tornadoes.

We also have climate scientists, who look at the big picture of how tornadoes fit into our planet's overall climate system. They study patterns over many years to see if and how things like climate change might be affecting tornado activity. Their work is like piecing together a giant jigsaw puzzle of our planet's climate.

Another group of experts are the emergency management professionals. These are the people who plan and coordinate responses to disasters, including tornadoes. They work on creating evacuation plans, setting up emergency shelters, and making sure communities are prepared for severe weather. They're like the captains of the ship, steering us safely through stormy weather.

For kids like Emily and Max, learning about these tornado experts was incredibly exciting. It showed them that studying tornadoes isn't just about being out in the field; it's about science, technology, engineering, and most importantly, helping people.

One of the coolest things about these scientists is how they work together. Meteorologists, engineers, climate scientists, and emergency managers all share information and ideas. It's like a super team, each member with their own special skills, working together to understand tornadoes and keep people safe.

But you know what? You don't have to be a grown-up to learn about tornadoes. Kids can be junior tornado detectives too! There are lots of fun and safe ways to learn about the weather. You can start a weather journal to keep track of the weather each day, make a simple rain gauge to measure rainfall, or even build a model of a tornado using a bottle.

The world of tornado science is always changing and growing. New discoveries are made all the time, thanks to the hard work of these tornado detectives. Their research helps us understand not just tornadoes, but the entire weather system of our planet.

tools of the trade

In the world of tornado research, scientists use some really cool and sophisticated tools. These tools help them understand how tornadoes form, move, and affect the environment. It's like having a super high-tech toolbox for exploring one of nature's most mysterious phenomena. Let's take a closer look at some of these amazing tools used in tornado research.

First on our list is the Doppler radar. This isn't your ordinary radar; it's like the superhero of weather radars! Doppler radar can detect precipitation, wind speed, and direction at different heights in the atmosphere. This is super important for understanding the conditions that lead to tornadoes. It works by sending out a pulse of energy and then measuring how that energy bounces back after hitting raindrops or other particles in the air. The way the energy returns tells meteorologists about the speed and direction of the wind within a storm. It's like having X-ray vision for the weather!

Another incredible tool is the weather balloon. These aren't just any balloons; they're specially designed to rise up to 100,000 feet in the atmosphere! Attached to these balloons are instruments called radiosondes, which measure temperature, humidity, and atmospheric pressure as they ascend. By sending up these balloons, scientists can get a vertical snapshot of the atmosphere, which helps them understand the conditions that could lead to severe weather, including tornadoes.

Then there's the Tornado Intercept Vehicle (TIV). This vehicle is like a tank meets a science lab. It's built to withstand high winds and flying debris, and it's equipped with all sorts of weather instruments. The TIV allows researchers to safely get close to tornadoes and collect data right from the heart of the storm. It has anemometers to measure wind speed, barometers for pressure, and even high-definition cameras to record everything. The TIV is like the ultimate storm-chasing machine!

But what about when tornado researchers can't get close to a tornado? That's where drones come in. Drones, or Unmanned Aerial Vehicles (UAVs), are becoming an important tool in tornado research. They can fly into places that are too dangerous for humans and collect data on temperature, humidity, and wind patterns. This helps scientists understand the structure of tornadoes and the environment around them. Drones are like the scouts of tornado research, going out to gather crucial information.

One of the most interesting tools used in tornado research is the mobile mesonet. These are vehicles equipped with weather instruments that can be driven around the edges of a storm. They measure things like wind speed, temperature, and humidity at ground level, giving researchers a detailed picture of the conditions near a tornado. It's like having a weather station on wheels!

Then there's LIDAR, which stands for Light Detection and Ranging. This tool uses laser light to measure distances and can create detailed 3D maps of tornado paths. By analyzing these maps, scientists can learn about the intensity and the damage patterns of tornadoes. LIDAR is like the artist of tornado research, painting a detailed picture of a tornado's impact.

For kids like Emily and Max, learning about these tools was an adventure in itself. It showed them how science and technology come together to help us understand and prepare for tornadoes. They imagined being tornado researchers themselves, using these tools to unravel the mysteries of the weather.

In addition to these high-tech tools, there's one more essential element in tornado research: observation. Tornado researchers spend a lot of time simply watching the sky, noting changes in cloud formations and wind patterns. This might seem simple, but it's a crucial part of understanding how tornadoes behave.

The tools of tornado research are like keys that unlock the secrets of these powerful storms. Each tool provides valuable information that helps build a bigger, clearer picture of how tornadoes form and what we can do to stay safe when they occur.

storm chasing

Have you ever wondered what it would be like to chase a tornado? For some people, this is more than just a wonder – it's a passion, a science, and an adventure.

Storm chasing is the pursuit of severe weather,

whether it's thunderstorms, tornadoes, or even supercells, by researchers, meteorologists, and thrill-seekers. It involves tracking and following these weather phenomena to understand them better or simply to experience their raw power and beauty.

Imagine you're in a car equipped with all kinds of gadgets – weather radar, GPS, and communication tools. The sky ahead is dark and swirling. You're driving towards it, not away. This is what storm chasing is all about. It's a mix of science, adventure, and a deep respect for nature.

The primary goal for many storm chasers is to collect data. Scientists and researchers chase storms to understand how they form and behave. This information is crucial for improving weather forecasts and tornado warnings, which ultimately helps save lives. For example, data collected by storm chasers can help meteorologists understand wind patterns in a tornado or how a storm evolves.

But it's not just about the data. For many chasers, there's a profound fascination with the beauty and power of storms. Tornadoes, with their immense energy and unique formations, are nature's incredible spectacles. Storm chasers often talk about the awe they feel watching these phenomena, a mix of reverence and excitement.

Storm chasing requires a lot of skill and knowledge. Chasers need to understand weather patterns and be able to interpret radar data to predict where a storm will go. It's like being a detective, looking for clues in the sky and the weather data to find the storm. They also need to be skilled drivers, able to navigate roads quickly and safely, often in challenging conditions.

Safety is a top priority in storm chasing. Experienced chasers know how to keep a safe distance from severe weather. They understand the risks and are always prepared to change plans if a storm becomes too dangerous. It's a delicate balance between getting close enough to observe and staying far enough to stay safe.

Storm chasing technology has come a long way. Today's chasers use sophisticated equipment like mobile radar units, high-resolution cameras, and drones. This technology allows them to capture detailed data and stunning images of storms, contributing valuable information to weather research.

Storm chasing also plays an important role in education and public awareness. Many chasers share their experiences and findings through documentaries, social media, and public speaking. This helps people understand the power of weather and the importance of being prepared for severe storms.

Some storm chasers even work with emergency services, providing real-time information about storms that can help in disaster response. Their reports from the field can give communities precious time to take shelter or evacuate if necessary.

The world of storm chasing is not just about the thrill of the chase. It's about a passion for understanding the weather, a commitment to safety, and a desire to help others. It's a unique blend of adventure and science, where every chase brings new knowledge and a deeper respect for the incredible forces of our planet.

5 / the impact of tornadoes on nature

environmental effects

WHEN WE THINK OF TORNADOES, we often picture the destruction they cause in towns and cities. But tornadoes also interact with natural landscapes in fascinating ways. They can carve paths through forests, change the course of rivers, and even create new ecosystems.

Let's start with forests. When a tornado barrels through a wooded area, it can uproot trees, snap trunks, and strip leaves and branches. This sudden change creates what scientists call a 'tornado alley' in the forest – a clear path where the tornado traveled. But this isn't just destruction. These openings in the forest can become hotbeds for new growth. Sunlight reaches the forest floor, allowing different types of plants to grow. It's like the tornado is an artist, clearing a canvas for new nature artwork to emerge.

Tornadoes can also affect rivers and lakes. When they pass over water bodies, they can stir up sediment from the bottom, changing water quality and affecting aquatic life. If a tornado is strong enough, it can even alter the course of small rivers or create new water channels. It's as if the tornado is playing a game of rearranging the landscape, moving water and earth to new locations.

In grasslands and prairies, tornadoes can have a surprisingly beneficial effect. By removing old or overgrown vegetation, they can stimulate the growth of new plants, maintaining the health of these ecosystems. This is similar to the role of wildfires in nature – clearing out the old to make way for the new.

• • •

Tornadoes can also create temporary habitats for wildlife. The gaps in forests and changes in water bodies can attract different species, some of which may not usually be found in that area. It's like the tornado is inviting new guests to the environment party.

Another interesting aspect is how tornadoes can impact soil. The intense winds can transport soil from one place to another, sometimes enriching poor soil areas with nutrients from richer soils. This natural mixing of soils can benefit agricultural lands, albeit in a very unpredictable and uncontrolled way.

The environmental effects of tornadoes aren't always positive, though. In urban areas, tornadoes can create large amounts of debris from destroyed buildings and infrastructure. This debris can harm natural habitats and pollute waterways. Cleaning up and managing this debris is a crucial part of post-tornado environmental care.

• • •

Tornadoes also remind us of the delicate balance in nature. They show us that even though they can be destructive, there's a rhythm and a cycle to everything in the environment. The aftermath of a tornado offers a unique chance for scientists to study how ecosystems recover and adapt after such intense disturbances.

animal responses

Imagine you're in a forest, and a tornado is forming nearby. Birds suddenly stop singing, squirrels scurry to their nests, and even the fish in the streams seem to dive deeper. Animals have various instinctual responses to changes in weather, including the drop in atmospheric pressure and the vibrations from low-frequency sounds that tornadoes produce. These natural alerts cue them to seek shelter or flee the area.

Birds, known for their keen sensitivity to weather changes, often react first. They may fly to safer areas or seek shelter in denser foliage. It's like they have a built-in weather radar, alerting them to danger. Scientists have observed significant changes in bird behavior and migration patterns in response to storm activity.

Squirrels, rabbits, and other small mammals also have their ways of dealing with tornado threats. They tend to hide in their burrows or find other safe spots. These tiny creatures are experts at sensing danger, often reacting before the tornado is visible.

Even aquatic animals react to tornadoes. Fish and amphibians are sensitive to changes in water pressure, which can be affected by the intense atmospheric pressure changes caused by a tornado. They might swim to the bottom of their habitats or hide under rocks. It's as if they know the water isn't safe when the skies turn angry.

Farm animals, too, show signs of distress when a tornado is near. Cows and horses might become restless, pacing and neighing or mooing more than usual. Farmers often can tell that something's up by watching their animals' behavior.

. . .

But what about pets? Dogs and cats are known to behave oddly before a tornado. They might hide, whine, or act more clingy than usual. This is likely because they can hear the low-frequency sounds of an approaching tornado, which are too low for human ears. For pets, this strange, unsettling noise can be a signal that something is wrong.

Then there are the stories of animals finding their way back home after a tornado has passed. Despite the chaos and the changed landscape, dogs and cats have been known to travel miles to return to their families. It's a testament to their incredible sense of direction and attachment to their homes and humans.

In the aftermath of a tornado, wildlife can face significant challenges. Their habitats might be destroyed, leaving them without food or shelter. But nature is resilient. New growth after a tornado can provide fresh habitats and food sources. Animals adapt to these changes, finding new ways to survive and thrive.

• • •

For kids like Emily and Max, learning about how animals respond to tornadoes is not only fascinating but also a lesson in the interconnectedness of nature. They realized that every creature, big or small, has its own way of dealing with the forces of nature.

Understanding animal behavior during tornadoes is also important for scientists. It helps them learn more about how animals perceive and react to severe weather. This knowledge can even assist in improving human responses to tornadoes.

As we delve into the world of animals and tornadoes, we're reminded of the incredible instincts and adaptations of wildlife. It shows us that, in the face of nature's most formidable events, the animal kingdom has its own set of survival strategies, honed by centuries of coexistence with the planet's dynamic weather systems.

6 / creative corner

tornado experiments

TORNADOES, with their swirling winds and mysterious nature, are fascinating to study. But how can we safely explore these powerful phenomena? The answer lies in fun, simple experiments that can help us understand the dynamics of tornadoes right at home. In this section, we'll dive into some safe and exciting tornado experiments that kids like Emily and Max, and perhaps you too, can try out.

1. The Classic Bottle Tornado

. . .

This is a classic experiment that demonstrates how a tornado's vortex forms. You'll need two 2-liter clear plastic soda bottles, water, duct tape, and glitter or food coloring (for effect).

- Fill one bottle about three-quarters full with water. Add a few drops of food coloring or some glitter.

- Place the empty bottle upside down on top of the water-filled one and tape them together at the necks, making sure the seal is tight.

- Turn the bottles so the one with water is on top, and give it a vigorous circular swirl as you turn it upside down.

- Watch as a mini tornado forms in the bottle as the water drains into the bottom bottle.

2. Tornado in a Jar

This experiment is similar to the bottle tornado but on a smaller scale. You'll need a large glass jar, water, dish soap, and vinegar.

• • •

- Fill the jar three-quarters full with water.

- Add a teaspoon of dish soap and a teaspoon of vinegar to the water.

- Swirl the jar in a circular motion. You'll see a vortex form in the center, resembling a tornado.

3. Tornado with Two Fans

This experiment requires two box fans, a few ping pong balls, and a misting bottle of water.

- Place the two fans facing each other, about five feet apart.

- Turn on the fans to medium speed and place a ping pong ball between them. The ball should hover in the air.

- Lightly mist the air above the ping pong ball. You'll see the mist twist in a vortex shape between the fans, simulating how air moves in a tornado.

4. Tornado Sound Effects

• • •

Understanding the sounds of a tornado can be as important as seeing one. For this, you need a long piece of thin, flexible metal sheeting and a pair of gloves.

- Hold the metal sheet by one end and shake it rapidly back and forth.

  - The fluttering sound resembles the low rumble of a tornado. This helps understand how low-frequency sounds are associated with tornadoes.

5. Heat and Tornado Formation

Tornadoes often form in warm conditions. This experiment illustrates that concept. You'll need a large clear plastic box, a small electric fan, red and blue food coloring, and two small, shallow dishes.

- Fill one dish with hot water and add red food coloring, and the other with cold water and blue coloring.

  - Place the dishes at opposite ends of the plastic box.

- Turn the fan on low and aim it towards the box. Watch how the colored mists (representing hot and cold air) interact and swirl, demonstrating how different air temperatures can create a vortex.

6. DIY Anemometer

Understanding wind speed is a big part of tornado science. In this experiment, you'll make a simple anemometer, a device used to measure wind speed. You need four small paper cups, two straws, a pin, a pencil with an eraser, and a stapler.

- Staple the straws together in a cross shape.
- Attach a cup to each end of the straw cross, making sure all the cups face the same direction.
- Push the pin through the center of the cross and into the pencil's eraser, allowing it to spin freely.
- Blow on the cups or hold your anemometer in the wind to see it spin, mimicking how an anemometer measures wind speed.

• • •

Each of these experiments brings a piece of tornado science to life. They help us understand the forces at play in these natural phenomena. For Emily and Max, these experiments turned their curiosity about tornadoes into exciting, hands-on learning experiences.

art and stories

Picture this: a classroom or a home, where kids are gathered around tables with crayons, markers, and paper. Some are busy writing, their pens creating worlds on paper, while others are deep into drawing, their hands moving in swirls and dashes as they bring tornadoes to life in their art.

The Power of Drawing

Drawing is a fantastic way for kids to express their thoughts and emotions about tornadoes. It's a visual exploration of what they've learned and how they feel. Here's how Emily and Max, along with their friends, dive into this creative process:

• • •

1. Drawing the Science: They start by drawing the structure of a tornado, from the swirling funnel to the debris cloud at the base. This helps solidify their understanding of how tornadoes look and work.

2. Emotional Expression: Some kids use colors to express how tornadoes make them feel. Dark, brooding colors for the power and destruction; bright, hopeful colors for the clear skies after the storm.

3. Tornado Stories: They draw scenes of tornadoes impacting landscapes, like a tornado over a farm or a city. This helps them understand and empathize with the effects of tornadoes on different environments.

The Magic of Storytelling

Writing stories is another great way for children to process what they've learned about tornadoes. It encourages them to use their imagination and build narratives around these whirlwind wonders.

• • •

1. Adventure Stories: Some kids write tales of adventure, where characters experience a tornado and learn important lessons about bravery and resilience.

2. Informative Narratives: Others write informative stories, weaving facts about tornadoes into a narrative, perhaps about a young meteorologist or a family preparing for a storm.

3. Mythical Tornado Tales: Inspired by the myths and legends discussed earlier, some children create their own mythical stories, personifying tornadoes and giving them characters and motives.

Combining Art and Writing

Why not combine both? Here's where the real fun begins.

1. Comic Strips: Kids create comic strips, narrating a story with pictures and words. These can be educational (explaining how tornadoes form) or purely imaginative (superheroes saving the day from a tornado).

2. Illustrated Stories: They write short stories or

poems about tornadoes and illustrate them. This could be a story about a family's experience during a tornado or a poem about the beauty and power of nature.

Reflecting and Sharing

At the end of their creative session, Emily, Max, and their friends share their art and stories. This sharing is an important part of the process. It allows kids to see different perspectives and understandings of tornadoes. It's a moment of connection and empathy, as they listen to each other's experiences and expressions.

1. Gallery Walk: They do a gallery walk, where drawings are displayed around the room, and kids walk around, looking at each other's work, discussing and asking questions.

2. Story Time: They gather in a circle for a story time, where those who want to can read their stories aloud. This fosters a sense of community and shared experience.

• • •

The Bigger Picture

Through drawing and writing, children like Emily and Max not only consolidate their learning about tornadoes but also develop their creativity and emotional intelligence. They learn to articulate their thoughts and feelings in various forms, a skill that goes beyond the classroom or the topic of tornadoes.

7 / myths and legends about tornadoes

tornado myths

MYTH 1: Tornadoes Can't Cross Rivers or Mountains

One of the most persistent myths is that tornadoes can't cross rivers or climb over mountains. Some people believe that the water in a river cools the air, weakening the tornado, or that mountains are just too big for a tornado to get over. But in reality, tornadoes don't mind getting their feet wet or climbing high. Rivers and mountains do not significantly impact the path or the power of a tornado. Tornadoes have been known to cross major rivers like the Mississippi and climb over mountain ranges. It's all about the atmospheric conditions, not the obstacles on the ground.

Myth 2: Opening Windows Reduces Damage

This myth suggests that opening windows in your house can equalize the pressure during a tornado, preventing the house from exploding. However, this is not true. Opening windows does nothing to prevent damage and can actually increase the risk of injury and damage by allowing wind and debris to enter the house. The best action is to leave the windows closed and find a safe place to shelter.

Myth 3: The Southwest Corner of a Basement is the Safest Spot

Many people grew up hearing that the southwest corner of a basement is the safest place during a tornado. The theory was that since tornadoes typically come from the southwest, debris would be less likely to fall in this corner. However, tornadoes can come from any direction, and debris can be blown in all directions. The safest place is actually under a sturdy piece of furniture or a mattress, away from windows and outside walls.

Myth 4: Tornadoes Don't Happen in Big Cities

There's a misconception that big cities are immune to tornadoes, perhaps because of the tall buildings or the heat of the city. But this is just a myth. Tornadoes can and do hit cities. The reason it seems rare is that cities occupy a small fraction of the land area, so the chances are statistically lower. But when they do strike urban areas, the damage can be extensive because of the high concentration of buildings and people.

Myth 5: Tornadoes Are Always Visible

Many people think of tornadoes as always being visible, giant funnels reaching from the sky to the ground. However, not all tornadoes are visible. Sometimes the tornado funnel is obscured by rain or low-hanging clouds. Other times, the tornado might not pick up enough debris or moisture to be seen. This is why relying on sight alone is not a safe way to judge the presence of a tornado.

Myth 6: You Can Outrun a Tornado in a Car

The idea of outrunning a tornado in a car is a dangerous misconception. Tornadoes can change direction quickly and unpredictably, and they can move faster than any car, especially through congested areas. The safest course of action if you're in a car is to drive to the nearest shelter. If that's not possible, it's safer to leave the car and seek shelter in a low-lying area like a ditch.

Myth 7: Tornadoes Only Happen in the Spring

While it's true that tornadoes are most common in the spring, they can occur at any time of the year if the conditions are right. Tornadoes have been recorded in every month of the year. They're not just a springtime phenomenon; they're a year-round concern.

tornadoes in folklore

In every corner of the world, people have looked up at the swirling skies and created stories about tornadoes. These tales, passed down through generations, are woven with wonder, awe, and sometimes a little fear. Let's embark on a storytelling journey around the globe to explore how different cultures have interpreted the mysterious and powerful tornado.

The Wind Spirits of Native America

In many Native American cultures, tornadoes were seen as the work of powerful wind spirits. For the Lakota people, the tornado was associated with Wakinyan, a powerful thunderbird. According to their belief, these thunderbirds were enormous creatures who lived in the clouds, and their wings caused thunder. When they were angry, they would descend to Earth as tornadoes, creating havoc with their powerful wings.

In the Choctaw tradition, tornadoes were linked to an angry spirit called Holla. The legend says that Holla would appear as a whirling tornado to punish those who offended him. These stories were not just tales of fear; they were reminders of respect for nature and its power.

The Dragon Twisters of China

In ancient China, tornadoes were often depicted as dragons. This was because the shape and movement of a tornado resembled that of a dragon moving through the sky. Chinese folklore is filled with tales of these dragon twisters, which were believed to be both powerful and capricious. The dragons were respected as controllers of the weather, capable of bringing both life-giving rains and destructive storms.

The Wind Demons of Japan

In Japanese folklore, tornadoes were sometimes associated with Fūjin, the god of the wind. He was depicted carrying a large bag of winds on his shoulders, unleashing them upon the world. When angered, Fūjin would let out the winds in the form of tornadoes, demonstrating his might and power. These stories were often told to explain the sudden and unpredictable nature of tornadoes.

The Whirling Djinn of the Middle East

In some Middle Eastern stories, tornadoes were thought to be caused by djinn, supernatural beings made of smokeless fire. These djinn were said to have the power to create powerful whirlwinds and sandstorms. They were often depicted as being mischievous or even malevolent, using their powers to confuse and frighten travelers.

The Cyclone Serpents of Australia

Australian Aboriginal mythology often speaks of the Rainbow Serpent, a powerful and revered spirit that's associated with water and rain. In some stories, this serpent is also linked to cyclones and tornadoes. The Rainbow Serpent's movement across the land was said to create the landscape, carving out rivers and valleys. When angered, it would show its power through violent storms and tornadoes.

The Storm Hags of Europe

European folklore, particularly from the British Isles, often featured storm hags – fierce, witch-like beings who could control the weather. These hags were said to ride the winds of storms, and in some stories, they created tornadoes. They would sweep across the countryside, causing destruction with their tempests.

Telling Tornado Tales

8 / conclusion

AS WE COME to the end of our tornado journey, it's a great time to look back and reflect on all the amazing things we've learned about these powerful forces of nature. From understanding the science behind tornadoes to exploring their impact on communities and cultures, our adventure has been both enlightening and exciting.

The Science of Tornadoes

We started our journey by diving into the science of tornadoes. We learned how these twisting columns of air form when warm, moist air collides with cold, dry air, creating a spinning effect due to changes in wind direction and speed with altitude. We explored different types of tornadoes, from the classic cone-shaped twisters to the rare waterspouts that dance over water.

Tornado Safety and Preparedness

Our adventure also taught us the importance of safety and preparedness. We discovered the best places to seek shelter during a tornado, like basements or interior rooms on the lowest floor, and we debunked common myths, like the idea that opening windows can lessen damage. We even learned how to make our own tornado emergency kits, packed with essential items like water, non-perishable food, and first-aid supplies.

The Impact on Communities

We saw how tornadoes can dramatically change landscapes and communities. They can carve paths through forests, create new ecosystems, and unfortunately, sometimes cause destruction in towns and cities. But we also learned about the resilience of communities, how people come together to rebuild and support each other in the aftermath of a storm.

Tornadoes in Culture and Myth

Our journey took a creative turn as we explored tornadoes in folklore and storytelling. We saw how different cultures have interpreted tornadoes in their myths and legends, from the wind spirits of Native America to the storm hags of Europe. We even encouraged kids to express their own understanding and feelings about tornadoes through drawing and writing, blending science with creativity.

The Roles of Experts

We met the experts who study tornadoes – meteorologists, storm chasers, engineers, and more. These tornado detectives use a range of tools, from Doppler radars to weather balloons, to understand and predict tornado behavior, helping to keep us safe.

The Animal World and Tornadoes

In a twist, we discovered how animals react to tornadoes. From birds falling silent before a storm to pets acting unusually, animals have their own ways of sensing and responding to the changes in the atmosphere brought by tornadoes.

Hands-on Experiments

We even got our hands dirty with some fun, safe experiments to simulate tornadoes and understand their dynamics. From creating a tornado in a bottle to making a DIY anemometer, these activities brought the science of tornadoes to life in an interactive way.

Summing Up the Whirlwind

As we close this book, it's clear that tornadoes are more than just weather events; they are a blend of science, nature, culture, and human experience. They remind us of the power of the natural world and the importance of respecting and understanding it.

call to action

One of the best ways to continue learning about tornadoes is to become a weather watcher. This doesn't mean just looking out the window (although that's a good start). It means paying attention to weather forecasts, understanding weather patterns, and observing how changes in weather affect the environment around you. You can even keep a weather diary, noting down different weather conditions each day and how they change.

Experiment and Explore

Don't forget the fun experiments we talked about! You can always try new experiments or even come up with your own. How about building a more complex weather station, or experimenting with different ways to create a vortex? The key is to keep asking questions and looking for answers. Remember, every great scientist started with a simple question: "Why?"

Be a Storyteller

Your stories and drawings about tornadoes are not just creative exercises; they're ways to process and share your understanding. Keep writing stories or creating art about the weather and nature. Maybe you can even start a blog or a small neighborhood newspaper with weather updates and stories. Your creativity can inspire others to learn and care about the environment.

Get Involved in Community Preparedness

Learning about tornadoes isn't only about understanding the science; it's also about knowing how to stay safe. Share what you've learned with your family and friends. Maybe you can help organize a tornado drill at school or create an emergency preparedness plan for your neighborhood. By taking action, you help create a community that's better prepared for tornadoes and other natural disasters.

Connect with Nature

Understanding tornadoes also means appreciating the broader environment. Spend time in nature, observe how different weather conditions affect the plants and animals, and learn about local ecosystems. This connection with nature will give you a deeper appreciation of the delicate balance of our planet.

Learn from the Experts

There are so many resources out there to continue your learning journey. Visit science museums, attend talks by meteorologists, or participate in local science fairs. Many universities and research institutions have outreach programs where scientists share their knowledge with the public. You might even get to meet a storm chaser or a weather researcher!

Use Technology to Your Advantage

In today's digital age, there's a wealth of information available online. Follow reputable weather websites, join online science clubs, or participate in interactive webinars about meteorology. There are also numerous educational apps and games that make learning about weather both fun and informative.

Think About the Future

As you learn more about tornadoes and the environment, start thinking about how you can contribute to the world. Maybe you'll become a meteorologist, an environmental scientist, or a climate change activist. Or perhaps you'll invent new technologies to predict weather or help reduce the impact of natural disasters. The possibilities are endless!

Spread the Word

Last but not least, be an ambassador for tornado awareness and safety. Share your knowledge with others, encourage your friends and family to be prepared, and be a voice for environmental conservation. Your enthusiasm can make a real difference in how your community views and responds to tornadoes and other natural phenomena.

Our journey through the world of tornadoes has been filled with learning, discovery, and creativity. As we end this chapter, remember that this is just the beginning of a lifelong adventure in learning and exploration. The world is full of wonders waiting to be discovered, and you have the curiosity, creativity, and courage to explore them. Keep asking questions, keep seeking answers, and keep sharing your knowledge. The future is bright with young minds like yours leading the way. So go forth, young explorers, and embrace the whirlwind of possibilities that awaits you!

9 / glossary and additional resources

ATMOSPHERIC PRESSURE: This is the weight of the air in the atmosphere. It can change depending on the weather and is a key factor in storm formation. Imagine the air above you as a giant ocean; the deeper you go, the more it presses on you. That's atmospheric pressure.

Anemometer: This is a tool used to measure wind speed. It's like a wind speedometer. Anemometers can be simple, like cups spinning on a pole, or more complex, like electronic devices.

Condensation: This happens when water vapor in the air cools down and changes back into liquid water. It's like when your cold glass of lemonade gets all sweaty on a hot day. That sweat is water vapor from the air condensing on the cold glass.

Doppler Radar: This is a special type of radar

used to study weather. It measures the speed and direction of objects, like raindrops, which helps meteorologists understand storm movement. It's like having super-sonic ears that can hear raindrops moving.

Fujita Scale (F-Scale): This scale measures tornado intensity based on the damage they cause. It ranges from F0 (weakest) to F5 (strongest). It's like a tornado report card, grading how powerful a tornado is.

Meteorologist: This is a scientist who studies the weather. They use data from radars, satellites, and other instruments to predict the weather. Think of them as weather detectives, solving the mysteries of the atmosphere.

Supercell: This is a highly organized type of thunderstorm. Supercells are often responsible for producing severe weather, including tornadoes. They're like the big bosses of storm world.

Tornado Alley: This is a region in the United States where tornadoes are most frequent. It includes parts of Texas, Oklahoma, Kansas, and Nebraska. It's like the favorite playground for tornadoes.

Tornado Watch: This means that conditions are right for a tornado to form. It's like a heads-up notification, saying, "Stay alert, tornadoes could happen."

Tornado Warning: This is issued when a tornado has been sighted or indicated by weather radar. It means, "Take cover now, a tornado is here or coming soon!"

Vortex: This is the spinning, swirling motion of air in a tornado or other storm. Think of it like the whirlpool you see when water goes down the drain, but way more powerful.

Waterspout: This is a tornado that forms over water. They're like water-dancing cousins of land tornadoes.

resources

Websites for Weather Whizzes

1. National Weather Service (weather.gov): The NWS website is a treasure trove of weather information, including up-to-date weather warnings, educational resources, and detailed explanations of weather phenomena.

2. NOAA's SciJinks (scijinks.gov): This interactive website, hosted by the National Oceanic and Atmospheric Administration, is all about weather. It's perfect for kids and teens, offering games,

videos, and fun facts about all things meteorological.

3. The Tornado Project (tornadoproject.com): This website is dedicated to providing information on tornadoes. It includes tornado myths, personal accounts, and data on past tornadoes.

4. Sky Diary (skydiary.com): Run by storm chaser Chris Kridler, this site offers a personal look at storm chasing, with photos, videos, and diary entries from her tornado-chasing adventures.

Apps for Storm Trackers

1. RadarScope (Available on iOS and Android): This app provides real-time radar data, ideal for those interested in tracking storms and understanding radar imagery.

2. Tornado by American Red Cross (Available on iOS and Android): This app offers alerts, safety tips, and real-time tornado information, making it a great tool for preparedness and education.

Documentaries for Visual Learners

1. "Tornado Alley": This documentary follows storm chasers as they pursue tornadoes in the Midwest. It's both educational and thrilling, offering a close-up look at tornado research in action.

2. "NOVA: Inside the Megastorm": This PBS documentary examines the formation and impact

of superstorms, including detailed analyses of storm systems.

Local Libraries and Museums

Don't forget about your local library and science museums! Many libraries have a wealth of books on weather and meteorology, and science museums often have exhibits on weather, including tornadoes.